2019 Poetry Challenge

Chemistry

L. Frank Baum's Land of Oz

Tricube

INTRODUCTION

Highland Park Poetry, founded in 2007, is dedicated to sharing poetry with audiences through our website as well as community events, writing workshops and poetry displays. Each year, Highland Park Poetry issues a Poetry Challenge to spark the imaginations of poets of all ages and levels – from experienced, published authors to beginning writers; from adults to students.

For the 2019 Poetry Challenge, participants were given three options: write about Chemistry (*recognizing the 150th anniversary of Dmitri Mendeleev's Periodic Table of Elements*), L. Frank Baum's Land of Oz (*recognizing the 100th anniversary of his death and the 80th anniversary of the MGM film The Wizard of Oz starring Judy Garland*), or write a Tricube poem, a form created by Philip Larrea. The Tricube consists of three verses of three lines each containing only three syllables. Poems were selected by our guest judges. British poet Laura Potts judged all the poems about chemistry. Texas poet Sylvia Riojas Vaughn made the selections for the poems about the Land of Oz. Past Virginia Poet Laureate Sofia Starnes chose the Tricube poems. We thank all of the poets who shared their writing with us. We thank the many teachers who encouraged their students to participate. We thank our guest judges for their time, energy and enthusiasm for the project.

Highland Park Poetry also wishes to thank the following individuals and organizations for their support of the 2019 Poetry Challenge:

- Photography by Lynn West, Bev Sykes and Kim Bernardi used on this book's cover
- Coffee Speaks & The Art Center of Highland Park for hosting our readings and events
- Youth Services Department at the Highland Park Public Library for encouraging student participation and hosting the Student Reading & Recognition.

Enjoy!

Sincerely,

Jennifer Dotson
Founder & Coordinator

www.HighlandParkPoetry.org

Contents

Enough Chemistry by Gail Denham 1

Baked In by Kerry Leaf 2

The Experiment by Ella Engelman 3

The Arc of Chemistry by Julie Isaacson 4

Ode to Argon by Kate Hutchinson 5

Big Explosion! by Reese Crosby 7

Chemistry by Emmie Dubin 8

Cavilaciones de una pasajera by Olivia Maciel Edelman 9

Ruminations of a Passenger by Olivia Maciel Edelman 11

Helium by Ed Werstein 13

The Periodic Table by Vladimir Kovalev..14

Sn by Khalid Mukhtar 15

101Md=Dmitry Mendeleev by Marjorie Rissman...16

Batrachotoxin by Everett Ciokajlo 17

So Many Elements! by Alessandra de Hayes 18

Paris, April 8, 1794 by Wilda Morris..19

After the Fall by Candace Kubinec 21

The Magic of Red Shoes by Marjorie Rissman 22

The Yellow Brick Road by Maddie Stevens 23

Oz by Megan Kim 24

Skipping Down the Yellow Brick Road by Marin Killeen 25

Oz by Abby Taub 26

Dmitry Antonovich Mendeleev and Lyman Frank Baum Converge Over the Rainbow by Emma Alexandra 27

Nick Chopper Lays Down His Axe by Ed Werstein 28

Scarecrow by Ellen Pickus...29

Curtains by Kerry Leaf...30

Oz by Sofia Fernandez...31

The Wizard of Oz by Emmett Heaton 32

The Wizard of Oz by Evan Peal...33

The Tinman by Elliot Shields 34

Lollipop Guild Builders by Julie Isaacson 35

Glinda Establishes the North Star Settlement House by Sylvia Cavanaugh.36

The Good Witch by Connie Vitale...37

Ruby Reds by Joseph Kuhn Carey 38

The Merry Old Land of Oz by Max Tarschis...39

The Wicked Witch Watching Me by Eden Gunsberg 40

Oz by Maddie Kashy...41

Wizard of Oz by Ben Brekher...42

Lessons of the Emerald City by Sophie Seligman...43

Dorothy Delivered by Kathleen A. Lawrence...44

vi

Oz by Grace Tipescu 45

the yellow brick road by Jael Nikiema 46

The Technique by Bill Lederer 47

Bird Watch by Carol Spielman Lezak 48

Horses by Lexi Peterson 49

Karate by Jacob Kaiserman 50

Paradise by Elliot Starkman 51

Apple River Canyon by Carol L. Gloor 52

Snowman by Max Pass 53

YouTube by Sammi Hoffberg 54

I See the Woods by Drake Elman 55

Earth by Noah Carson 56

New Year Dream by Marjorie Rissman 57

In San Miguel de Allende, 2007 by Wilda Morris 58

Sheltering by Merle Tovian 59

Nature's Dance by Emma Alexandra 60

What to Do? by Kathleen A. Lawrence 61

All That Remains by Jan Chronister 62

Hoover by Addison Dickman 63

Cake is Great by Shayna Itkin 64

A Girl's Game by Eden Bernardi 65

Strange Animals by Valentina Di Martino 66

Animals by Sadie Weissman...67

ABOUT THE JUDGES 69

CHALLENGE 1 - CHEMISTRY

Gail Denham – *1st Place, Adult Non-Resident*

Enough Chemistry

Aggie and Ralph date off and on
for three years. "There's good chemistry
a' tween you," says Ma. "Whyn't you make
it permanent? Ralph's a good steady fella."

"Chemistry, ha!," Aggie pouts. "More like
spontaneous combustion. Any little thing
makes him explode. Last night it was cuz
I ordered chicken instead of steak."

"Come on," Ralph groans. "Brought
you to this fancy restaurant and you order
chicken. You don't appreciate
what I do for you. Steak is their specialty."

Aggie giggles. "So I chewed real slow.
Every bite I either smacked my lips
or lifted the fork high so's he'd notice.
He was so irritated he gobbled
his steak. Thought maybe he'd choke."

"He didn't even kiss me good night,
he was so put out. Drove off fast.
Only a drop of acid and he'll blow
off his lid. He's a formula for disaster."

"Other day he grumbled for five minutes
cuz I went out ahead of him, didn't let him
open the door. And he doesn't like cats."

"Time I moved on to someone
who at least has some of the same
elements I do. Doncha' think, Ma?"

Kerry Ann Leaf – *1st Place, Highland Park Resident*

Baked In

When the weighted
Measure of
Sifted
Unbleached flour
And baking powder
And dark brown sugar
And sea salt
And Dutch cocoa
Play with
Beaten eggs
And milk
And luscious liquids
And live together
For an hour or so
In the warmth
Of their panned shelters,
The chemical magic outcome
Is awesome.

Ella Engelman – *1st Place, Elementary Student*

The Experiment

I mix and mix all day and night
Trying to get my potion just right.
"I am mad, I am evil," I told myself,
I took my recipe off the shelf.
I looked at the list then took a big gasp
I ran to get my oxygen mask.
I told myself, "Any minute now."
Suddenly I heard a big POW!

I screamed as the mixture flew over my head,
I thought I was about to be dead.
I closed my eyes and took a deep breath
Wishing to escape my death.
Minutes later I opened my eyes.
I looked around with total surprise.
I was living, I was breathing,
I wasn't even bleeding.

I realized the potion made a hole in my wall,
But I really didn't care at all.
I ran out of the lab,
I would never return.
No more chemistry, that's a good thing to learn.

Julie Isaacson – *2nd Place, Highland Park Resident*

The Arc of Chemistry

Chemistry. Vague measure of the subjective, variant depth
of a relationship.
The spark, the glue, the joy, the magnetic pull.

"Yes, there's all that questionable behavior, but we have CHEMISTRY."

And others nod knowingly, as if to say, "Ah, yes! The chemistry which forgives all
else."

Like cholesterol, there's good and bad chemistry.

When it's good, it's like H2O. Refreshing, vital, necessary to one's existence.
Provides
strength and sustenance.

If the chemistry is *really* good, the relationship is ignited with calcium chloride
and
potassium nitrate. FIREWORKS!

But alas, these compounds are not sustainable! Way too much maintenance.

The acids and bases must combine just right—all such a delicate balance.
Possibly
resulting in Neutral. Or worse...Hydrogen Fluoride. Don't be fooled by the old
trick
of salt combined with mercury thiocynate. It might be a lure for phosphine.

Chemistry—be careful, or one can get burned on the road from lust to combust.

And if the ex(periment) is spotted out on the street, one can say, "Eh..that one
didn't
know a mass from a mole in the ground."

Kate Hutchinson – *2nd Place, Adult Non- Resident*

Ode to Argon

Argon is an unusual element, rarely reacting with other elements to form compounds.

O argon of no intention! You were
born of cosmic rays to hover forever
like tiny pods near the mother ship.

O argon of the Tyrannosaur,
swimming in pillow-sized lungs
and exhaled into ancient atmospheres

to circulate all these million years!
Argonauts inhaled you back in Greece
and somehow claimed your name—

lazy, inactive—dubbed because you don't
mix it up with the other atoms. You're
singular, stand-offish— but complete.

To think! The same argon atoms I breathe
blew here from the ancients—Homer
and Aristophanes with a puff expelling

Priam's pain and Lysistrata's decree.
Attila the Hun inhaled you! And Joan
before she was of Arc, out gathering eggs,

and Will in his dusty office at the Globe
penning orisons for kings, and Whitman
yawping you into never-ending songs.

O argon, atomic acrobat—so deftly
snuffing out fires or stifling the lives
of ten thousand fowl a day for Purdue,

preserving our Constitution under
inch-thick glass, and cutting into flesh
in our surgeons' blue-green laser beams.

O Element 18, ten percent of this air!
You will ricochet among the roaches
when there are no more human lungs to fill.

Reese Crosby – *2nd Place, Elementary Student*

Big Explosion!

I had a great idea
For a special potion
I hope that nothing gets broken
I pour in some bam
I pour in some boom
I can't wait until it explodes all over the room!
I paint it brown
I paint it black
I make sure I paint the back
I put a little of this…
I put a little of that…
5
4
3
2
1
With a boom!
A bam!
A pow!
A shazam!
My volcano exploded
With a big loud WHAM!

Emmie Dubin – *3rd Place, Elementary Student*

Chemistry

Look around the lab for this and that.
Bags of toenails and cartons of scat.
Toxic, keep out, don't let that explode!
Eww! I found the head of a toad.

Watch out for that shelf!
Don't touch the monster fur.
Concoctions of things never seen before.
Hazardous boxes full of mystery things.
Crates filled to the brim with snake skins!

EEEKKK!! I let out a big scream.
I woke up, it was just a dream.

Olivia Maciel Edelman – *3rd Place, Highland Park Resident*

Cavilaciones de una pasajera

> *- Para Metra*
> *(Sistema de ferrocarril de usuarios en el área de Chicago)*

Viajeros de Metra, su atención por favor,
el próximo tren entrante llegará a la estación
en aproximadamente… cinco minutos
(Estación de Highland Park, Illinois)

Siemens y Alstom generarían dieciocho billones de dólares
      con su fusión.

Crispr / Cas9 es una prometedora técnica molecular
para editar el código genético.

Alguien cultiva bacterias sobre alambres metálicos
para agilizar el proceso fotosintético.

En Israel se ha descubierto un nuevo mineral azul,
      tan precioso como el zafiro;
se le ha llamado ¨carmelito¨
por haberse hallado en el área de Carmel.

¿Y qué del brillante descubrimiento
sobre el funcionamiento neuronal de Dn. José Ramón y Cajal?

¿Y qué de Babbage y de Ada Lovelace?

¿Y qué de la magnífica
Tabla Periódica de Dmitri Mendeleiév?

Enroscados, encerados,
los oscuros y helados desfiladeros de la noche
amenazan con tragarse a la tierra y sus océanos.
¿De qué nos servirá la ciencia
si olvidamos el ala beligerante y alumbrada del filosófo,
el ojo anímico del profeta,
la tierna y calenturienta caricia de la abuela en el hospicio?

Viajeros de Metra, su atención por favor,
el próximo tren saliente saldrá de la estación
en aproximadamente… cinco minutos
(Estación de Ogilvie, Chicago, Illinois).

Olivia Maciel Edelman – *3rd Place, Highland Park Resident*

Ruminations of a Passenger

> *- For Metra*
> *(Urban railroad system in the Chicago area for commuters)*

Metra commuters, your attention please,
the next inbound train will arrive into the station
in approximately… five minutes
(Train station, Highland Park, Illinois)

Siemens and *Alstom* would generate eighteen BN dollars
        with their merger.

Crispr / Cas9 is a promising molecular technique
to edit the genetic code.

Someone cultivates bacteria on metallic wires
to make photosynthesis more agile.

In Israel a new blue mineral has been discovered,
        as precious as sapphire,
called "carmelite", as it has been found in the area of Carmel.

And what about the brilliant discovery
by Dn. José Ramón y Cajal of the functioning of neurons?

And what about Babbage and Ada Lovelace?

And what about the magnificent
Periodic Table by Dmitry Mendeleev?

Curled upon themselves, waxed,
the darkened and frozen gorges of the night
threaten to swallow earth and its oceans.
Of what use will science be
if we forget the belligerent and illuminated
wing of the philosopher,
the anemic eye of the prophet,
the tender and feverish caress of grandmother in the hospice?

Metra commuters, your attention please,
the next outbound train will depart the station
in approximately... five minutes
(Ogilvie Station, Chicago, Illinois).

Ed Werstein – *3rd Place, Adult Non-Resident*

Helium

Your parents were a couple of hot heads
blew up at the drop of a match
that nasty Hindenberg incident
the most famous of the many times
they lost control.

But they found their matchmaker
in the sun god, your namesake.

When hydrogen atoms get close
and start feeling good about each other
things heat up in a hurry.

The hotter it gets, the closer they get.
They fuck, they fuse,
and are destroyed by their own passion.
Passing on all of their parts and none
of their traits, they become something
completely different: you.

You lead a long lineage of nobility,
a calm inertia is your greatest asset.

You are uplifting, rising
to every occasion,
great fun at parties.

People lift their voices
and speak very highly
of you.

Vladimir Kovalev – *Honorable Mention, Elementary Student*

The Periodic Table

Take hydrogen, carbon and some oxygen,
You get the thing you use every day,
Which is soap.
Now let's mix,
Carbon,
Chromium,
Nickel,
Molybdenum,
Manganese,
Silicon and copper,
Introgen and niobium.
Then go find the steel that has no stain,
Never damaged by the rain,
And that is the stainless steel.
Now let's mix some more.
Carbon,
Hydrogen,
Oxygen,
Nitrogen,
Chlorine,
And sulfur.
Go get a plastic bag and that is what it makes!

Khalid Mukthar – *Honorable Mention, Adult Non-Resident*

Sn

I can't stand
these heartless
men of tin

lying 'round
waiting for
tornado-

borne lasses
To save their...
Can't Stannum.

Marjorie Rissman – *Honorable Mention, Highland Park Resident*

101Md=Dmitry Mendeleev

no Nobel Prize for him
no vodka named after him
but element 101 and
a crater on the far side
of the dark moon
bear his name

a foreign member
of the Royal Society,
a bigamist banned from
Russian Academy of Science,
a dreamer who became
Father of the Periodic Table,

introduced the metric system to Russia,
a founder of the first oil refinery there,
teacher, author, chemist, scientist,
but unable to play the game,
the politics of the Nobel Prize
three times refused to honor him

who else claimed to dream their greatest
accomplishment, to write it down next
morning and find only one mistake in his
head or memory; all we know today is
the Table is the achievement of a genius,
leaving room for new elements to come.

Everett Ciokajlo – *Honorable Mention, Elementary Student*

Batrachotoxin

The scientist pulls in his driveway with his rickety car.
He lives away from the city, very far
He mixes two dangerous chemicals and does not know what it
will make.
He thinks they might just disintegrate and bake.
He is wrong, very wrong and he makes batrachotoxin
The test tube explodes and he is boxed in,
He cannot get out,
He fusses and pouts.
EVERYTHING EXPLODES!

Alessandra De Hayes – *Honorable Mention, Elementary Student*

So Many Elements!

Aluminum is all I can remember,
Since I learned the Periodic Table last December,
I've been stuck trying to figure out,
What atoms are all about.

Well just now, I learned about Rhuenium,
But I can't keep track of Selenium,
After I learned all the elements in the Periodic Table,
I'm starting to feel a little unstable!

Wilda Morris – *Honorable Mention, Adult Non-Resident*

Paris, April 8, 1794
In memory of Antoine Lavoisier

Blood spattered
the base
of the guillotine–

A head,
respiration stopped,
brain severed

from the hand
which recorded
ideas linking

his own experiments
with those of others,
building the basics

of modern chemistry,
wrote words urging reform
of prisons and hospitals,

handed out
his own funds
to feed people

in famine and poverty,
wrote against *pied forchu*
tax against Jews,

proposed fire hydrants,
schools for peasants,
better street lights.

Someone's head
should roll
for this base travesty.

First published in *The Iconoclast*, 91 (2006), p. 32.

CHALLENGE 2 – THE LAND OF OZ

Candace Kubinec – *1st Place, Adult Non-Resident*

After the Fall

The yellow brick road is
Full of weeds and
No one believes in the
Wonderful Wizard or
His magic any longer

Glinda the Good and the
Wicked Witch have
Opened a coffee bar
In downtown Oz –
No water is served

Dorothy has abandoned
Her ruby slippers and
Founded a rescue farm
For homeless Flying Monkeys

Only Toto remembers
The way home.

Marjorie Rissman – *1st Place, Highland Park Resident*

The Magic of Red Shoes

not the lion, the scarecrow, the tin man
although they were magical enough,
it was all about the shoes, the glittery
ruby slippers that Dorothy wore day after day,
night after night, when she went to Oz and when
she came home and saw Auntie Em again.

they were pure magic, from the tip of the toes
to the back of the heels, from the red outside
to the black sole and innersole. they walked
on the yellow brick road and beyond taking
this girl and her beloved puppy in the basket,
from her bed to see the wizard and home again,

once she learned that there is no other place
to want to be, because home is where love is
always waiting. So click your heels and say it loud
and clear and you too will walk in the red shoes
of Dorothy and visit the lion, the scarecrow, the
tin man, the Munchkins, the Good Witch,
 the

Bad Witch, and the Wizard but learn to come
back where it all began in the house that you
call home, in the bed where you grew up, where
hopefully you learned how to love and be loved.
remember that oz means courage in Hebrew,
a word you must take with you wherever you go.

Maddie Stevens – *1st Place, 4th Grade Student*

The Yellow Brick Road

The long stretch to get home,
A twisty, windy, curvy place,
A road that can lead to danger,
A forest frightening and scary.
This road is trick, so shiny too.
That **red ruby slippers** can dance down it
There you might find happiness and meet friends along the way,
It could lead you to a city,
So emerald and green,
The yellow brick road can't predict,
What's in store for you.
There might be a wicked witch,
So, get ready for the adventure,
Because this amazing road awaits...
...The Yellow Brick Road

Megan Kim – *1st Place, 5th Grade Student*

Oz

L. Frank Baum,
Creator of *The Wizard of Oz*
First, an introduction of the four friends
Whose journey is amazing beginning to end
Dorothy with her shoes so bright
The scarecrow with no brains try as he might
A Tin Man in need of a heart for his chest
A Lion longing for courage at its best
Their journey I know tells an elaborate story
No wonder the author is known with such glory
But how did he come up with such a concept
Maybe it started up in his office
His shelves were labeled, yes, indeed
From A to N
From O to Z
Then he decided
Oh, what a name!
Oz was perfect!
He thought in his brain
Maybe it started, beginning like that
But we'll never know
And the reason is sad
L. Frank Baum
creator of *The Wizard of Oz*
Died a hundred years ago
But his magical story
Will forever be told

Marin Killeen – *2nd Place, 4h Grade Student*

Skipping Down the Yellow Brick Road

The yellow brick road, the yellow brick road, what a wonderful place to be.
There I stand with glee, skipping down the yellow brick road I go.
In my red ruby slippers with all my friends, we all skip together to the end.
Click click click I dance down the yellow brick road with me in my slippers, and all
of my wonderful friends.

Abby Taub – *2nd Place, 5th Grade Student*

Oz

Over one hundred years of Oz,
The wonderful wizard of Oz.

First there is Dorothy,
Dorothy and her shoes.

Then there is the Scarecrow,
Looking for a brain.

Next up is the Tin Man,
Searching for a heart.

Finally the Lion,
Longing to be brave.

L. Frank Baum,
The creator of the magic,
He died 100 years ago.

But we will still remember,
The magic that he brought.

Emma Alexandra – *2nd Place, Highland Park Resident*

Dmitry Antonovich Mendeleev and Lyman Frank Baum Converge Over the Rainbow

And so, Mr. Baum, how extraordinary that we
should converge here, here over this, this
rainbow, rainbow the colors of our universe.
The atomic magnitude of this transport overwhelms me.

As it does me, Mr. Mendeleev, does me indeed... Elemental
in its composition, yet, monumental in its mystery, bit
magical I'd say. And, do call me Frank by the way. We,
Americans prefer the informality of first names.

With pleasure Frank. Dmitry, will do as well. You can skip
my patronymic, though Antonovich honors my father, Anton.
Temporary situation and location call for simplicity,
simplicity down to its lowest number in my periodic table.

Absolutely Dmitry, as simple as the air, the oxygen, we breathe.
We fly through time, as light as hydrogen filled dirigibles.
In our mid-thirties when we each achieved stardom in our own way.
You, with your Periodic Table of Chemical Elements.

I was 3 years old in 1869 when you, after hours, sleepless
nights, exhausted, dreaming, placed, and replaced,
your meticulously marked cards of chemical elements, your
game of solitaire, suits for horizontal, numbers for vertical.

Frank, with your book, *The Wonderful World of Oz*,
in 1900, you touched a chord. I was 66 years old then.
Could I create a chemical language as simple as the air,
the oxygen we breathe, understandable to a child of any age.

I thought to myself as I wrote children's books, could I teach
something as difficult as chemistry. Could I convert
your table, Dmitry, to a dance, a rhythmic affirmation of knowledge,
elemental in composition, monumental in mystery.

Ed Werstein – *2nd Place, Adult Non-Resident*

Nick Chopper Lays Down His Axe

The Tin Woodman, originally an ordinary man, Nick Chopper (the name first appeared in The Marvelous Land of Oz, by L. Frank Baum), used to make his living chopping down trees in the forests of Oz.

for Sylvia

I never saw the woods like this before
every tree sacred
the forest a cathedral.

Yesterday I spied her
a sprite, a spirited sylph
dancing in a clearing
around the altar
of a felled trunk.

I was blinded
like Paul on the Damascus Road
forever altered
forever her disciple.

And when my vision cleared
I gazed into the polished metal
of my axe and saw myself
real and true for the first time
a hollow man
heartless
as a money changer
in this wooded temple.

I am the Tin Man
whose tears of remorse
now rust my hinged joints.

I stand here motionless
empty
praying for holy oil
from the sylvan goddess
to liberate my dance of joy.

Ellen Pickus – *3rd Place, Adult Non-Resident*

Scarecrow

You've drawn my mouth tight shut.

Who wants to hear what you have to say?
You haven't got a brain in your head.

You've forced my arms onto a crucifix
offering no salvation,
frozen to scare others off,
to embrace no one.

And I can never leave your yard
to explore or learn
or meet any wizards,
true or false,

with my head stuck
in one direction
in a field of bitter green corn,
facing only one view—

the one you chose for me.

Kerry Leaf – *3rd Place, Highland Park Resident*

Curtains

Behind Tara's curtains
Stood manufactured glamor,
A living figure
Bedecked in handmade dress.

Behind the Iron Curtain
Stood countries divided,
A barrier
Built of ideological idiocies.

Behind the curtain of Oz
Stood hidden desires and hopes
That a wizard
Could whip the world into shape.

Behind all curtains of fear
Stand numbed scarecrows and lions and tin men
Yearning for a Dorothy
To show them the way.

Sofia Fernandez – *3rd Place, 5th Grade Student*

Oz

100+ years of Oz
4 characters in a story
Dorothy a world
away from home
Scarecrow looking for
A brain
The lion's courage that
knows its bounds
The Tin Man's heart that
was never there
100+ years of Oz
4 characters in
a story that will
be told forever

Emmett Heaton – *3rd Place, 4th Grade Student*

The Wizard of Oz

The man that needs the heart
Maybe the tin covered soulless machine
Lost his heart
Maybe he did not love
That was why he was not given a chance to have a heart
Maybe this cold heartless alien gave his heart to someone else
Who knows why the tin covered phenomenon
Doesn't have a heart.

Evan Peal – *Honorable Mention, 4th Grade Student*

The Wizard of Oz

Lions and Tigers and Bears, Oh My!
Run for your life and try not to cry!
Look at those monkeys fly!
We're off to see the Wizard
the wonderful Wizard of Oz

Come along and sing along
and walk the yellow brick road.
We're off to see the Wizard,
the wonderful Wizard of Oz.

The Cowardly Lion, Dorothy and
Tin Man, and don't forget about Scarecrow,
were all on their way to see the Wiz
to talk about their biz.

Until that wicked old witch tried to cast her spells on
the Lion, Scarecrow, Tin Man and Dorothy.
Then the witch was on her broom and came
to her Doom when the house fell on her head!
Ding Dong the witch is dead!

All the munchkins in the Land of Oz began to sing, sing a song in joy.
The Lion could search for his nerve, the Scarecrow could search for his brain,
the Tin Man may search for his heart and Dorothy how to go back home to
Kansas.

We're off to see the Wizard, the wonderful Wizard of Oz, because because
because because because the wonderful Wizard of Oz he was.

Elliot Shields – *Honorable Mention, 5th Grade Student*

The Tinman

Oil, Oil everywhere
with his silver shine and his sunny glare.
He has no heart, he has no hair,
But deep inside, the kindness is there.
With his bolts and his screws, he has some issues,
He meets three friends on the way that help him out in every way.

Julie Isaacson – *Honorable Mention, Highland Park Resident*

Lollipop Guild Builders
Give Us Your Trust, We'll Get On The Stick

Seventy-Five Years Experience
Bricklaying Created for your Special Desires
Originators of Yellow Brick, High Gloss or Matte Finish

Our Masons Offer Brains, Heart and Courage
In all Hardscapes and Commissions

In a Rush? We can drop in Fast
By Balloon or Flying Monkey Drones

It Doesn't Take a Wizard to Know Where to Call
Our Designs Will Make you Feel Like Dancing

Read the Reviews, or call 1-800-EMERALD for References
****
I was at my wit's end with previous contractors.
----Scarecrow

Their brick is strong enough to keep its shine under my heavy metal.
---- Tin Man

I'm not lyin' when I say this is the bravest walk I ever took.
---- Lion

I'd kill for a path like that.
----W.W.of W.

Their work was like magic! It was as though I waved a wand,
and it was done!
---Glinda

This beautiful path makes me feel every day that
There's No Place Like Home.
----Dorothy

What's Yellow?
----Toto

Sylvia Cavanaugh – *Honorable Mention, Adult Non-Resident*

Glinda Establishes the North Star Settlement House

It was the epiphany that flooded my brain as I spoke
to Dorothy about home. The realization that home
can be here, there, anywhere. Samwise carried
the Shire all the way to the flanks of Mount Doom.

Indeed, I studied abroad in Middle Earth my junior
year. I spent most of my time in Rivendell as the last
of the Elves prepared for their journey to the sea.
I realized early on I was in over my head, culturally,
but joined in singing ancient songs to the stars as
they rose in the night sky. Elrond praised my voice,
pure as starlight, and called me North Star.

I kept track of Dorothy after I sent her on her journey
down the yellow brick road. In my mind's eye, I saw
the gatekeeper of the Emerald City weep, then allow
the desperate travelers to pass through his tall gates.

Yes, this would be my city. When Dorothy left
I donned sea-green leggings and took the jade elf
cloak with silver star clasp from the old trunk in
the attic. The only glitter I wear is on my fingernails,
but the children love it, so I keep this one vanity.

The North Star welcomes the weary, the refugee,
the traveler from other lands, and speakers of foreign
tongues, like Munchkin, Monkey, and Elvish.

I've met the Winged Monkey King, hunkered down
In the forest, and our discussions show promise.

Connie Vitale *– Honorable Mention, Highland Park Resident*

The Good Witch

He used to call me Glinda
In the days of yore,
And Glinda was a good witch
If you give credence to the lore.

Her feet n'ere touched the ground,
She floated in a bubble.
In doing good she found delight.
Knew he not he was in trouble?

Sugar and spice and everything nice -
Wait … Kali is her middle name?!?
Oh how different it would be
If he only had a brain

Expecting patience and noblesse
Put the horse before the cart.
Oh how different it would be
If he only had a heart.

Tarnished halos weigh so heavy,
Being good a joyless scourge.
Oh how different it would be
If he only had some courage.

He used to call me Glinda
And my eye would start to twitch.
I tumbled from my pedestal
And now he calls me Witch.

Joseph Kuhn Carey – *Honorable Mention, Adult Non-Resident*

Ruby Reds

Those ruby slippers
have lived on in memory
because they can take you home
from colorful Oz to
a bleak black & white Kansas farm
or anywhere else you want to go
and isn't that where you'd choose
to go if you could
back to where warm meals are waiting
and the people and things you love in
present or past are stored, each
a touchstone in the deep well of family consciousness
that's molded you into the person you've become,
just three clicks and you're back
from wild and woolly adventures in the world
at large, and the twister's over and
plenty of familiar faces are crowding 'round,
welcoming you with open arms, smiles and love,
but the slippers will always be there,
up on a dusty closet shelf,
calling out to you to come back to Oz and
the glorious green Emerald City someday,
with all of that radiant, beautiful, shiny,
sparkling possibility and power packed in
those little old ruby reds.

Max Tarschis – *Honorable Mention, 4th Grade Student*

The Merry Old Land of Oz

Dorothy sat there poorly, in Black, White, and Gray.
But when things got all happy, this is all she could say.

Follow the yellow brick road! Follow the yellow brick road!
Out of the munchkins mouths' good songs flowed.

Along her journey she found lots of friends.
Along with some enemies that wanted to bring them all to their ends.

Lions, Tigers, Bears! Oh my!
Monkeys soaring through the sky!

Oh no! There is a witch!
My eyes are starting to twitch!

Ding Dong the witch is Dead!
By dumping water on her head!

Eden Gunsberg – *Honorable Mention, 4ᵗʰ Grade Student*

The Wicked Witch Watching Me

I stand in my shadow,
wondering, thinking.
It feels like the witch is looking at me over my shoulder,
watching every move I make, every step I take.

I take a step forward, the witch follows me.
I take a step backward, the witch follows me.
"Go away!" I scream, but she just won't go.

The witch is the cold winter storm
that no one ever looks forward to.
The witch is the screeching of the nails
when they scratch the chalkboard.
With the witch, I feel upset and lonely.
But you must not think about this witch.
You must always look
at the greener and sunnier side of the field;
the bright side.

You must think about all the colorful and beautiful creatures.
You must think wisely, courageously and most of all brightly.

Maddie Kashy – *Honorable Mention, 5th Grade Student*

Oz

Following a path,
We end up here just like that.
We see a scarecrow with a nice hat.
He talks, he walks, But no brain.

We see a big lion, furry my bravery he needs.
He asked can "I walk with you please."
We said yes he liked my blue dress.

We see a tin man, Frozen and stuck.
We give him a oil to unstuck him.

We walk, and walk till we see a door,
It's green. It scared me. I screamed.

Woah a castle, boom a witch my shoes she says.
We ran and ran, Boom bam.

Ben Brekher – *Honorable Mention, 5th Grade Student*

Wizard of Oz

A tornado caused me to land
on a witch's body,
met a tinman with no heart,
a scarecrow with no brain,
and a lion with no courage.
I gave a lion courage,
a robot a heart,
and taught a crow to think.

Sophie Seligman – *Honorable Mention, Highland Park Resident & High School Student*

Lessons of the Emerald City

Life is spinning,
Like I'm in a hurricane.
Do I need courage,
A heart,
Or brains?
So many questions,
That life may bring,
And decisions to make,
With every little thing.
But if you follow the bricks,
That glow a bright gold,
You may be able to conquer
The great unknown.
What's out there?
Lions, tigers, bears?
Oh my!
Or is it just like the sweet stories,
From my lullabies.
Will I reach Oz?
And when will I learn,
That I am the one who knows my future,
And the knowledge for which I yearn.
Not the man behind the curtain,
In some faraway land.
But me, a young girl,
With her heart in her hands.
Courage in her soul,
And a brain in her head,
I am the only one to attain my goals,
And take on the world ahead.

Kathleen A. Lawrence – *3rd Place, Adult Non-Resident*

Dorothy Delivered
(spiraling abecedarian)

Auntie Em
anxiously bellowed,
before the blowing, cartwheeling
country cyclone dumped Dorothy and her
dog efficiently.
Embarking far,
flying Gale with a gust
grounded on a half-hidden hag.
House now immobilized, an
iridescent image in jeweled globe joined the
jolly juveniles. Kansas
knew little of lilting ladies,
lollipop guilds, merry munchkins, and
menacing monkeys. Nevertheless, Glinda of the
North offered her an
offbeat option: Oz. Picking up pals,
powering through poppies, the quirky quartet
queued for their quest. Rallying, Dorothy
ran in ruby slippers with
Scarecrow, Scaredycat, Tinmman and Toto too,
trekking to urban Oz.
Unctuous Wiz in verdigris
vowed to value the Wicked Witch of the
West's broom. Water extinguished her
exploits. Yea-sayers yelled "to the
yellow brick road." Zonked gal
zoomed home.

Grace Tipescu – *Honorable Mention, 5th Grade Student*

Oz

We are off to see the wizard the wonderful wizard of Oz!
Dorothy with her red sparkly shoes woke up in a world called Oz.
Home
Scarecrow is longing for a brain, that will bring pride to his name.
Brain
Tin Man is wishing for a dove to bring him a heart to love.
Heart
The Cowardly Lion wishing for the courage to make all animals bow down at the
sight of him.
Courage
We thank the man that gave us Oz, the wonderful wizard of Oz!

Jael Nikiema – *Honorable Mention, 4th Grade Student*

the yellow brick road

walking down the yellow brick road
I saw the grass looking like it was mowed
the yellow brick road was shining
like the sun light towards Oz.

CHALLENGE 3 – TRICUBE

Bill Lederer – *1st Place, Adult Non-Resident*

The Technique

Who taught her
to be like
a goddess?

Her design
is as strong
as it gives.

Her web traps
others in
its wonder.

Carol Spielman Lezak – *1st Place, Highland Park Resident*

Bird Watch

The empty
pond shimmers
in the sun,

still and smooth,
until the
surface breaks

when a sleek
heron dives
in to eat.

Lexi Peterson – *1st Place, 5th Grade Student*

Horses

Click clop clop
On the trail
Break a stick

Scare a quail
Slip on mud
Jump a log

Run, trot, stop
All year long
Clop click clop

Jacob Kaiserman *– 1st Place, 4th Grade Student*

Karate

Downward block
Fist block down
Feet apart

Rising block
Blocking up
Fist on hip

Knife hand block
Hands open
Looking straight

Elliot Starkman – *2nd Place, Highland Park Resident & High School Student*

Paradise

I ran from
Home to find
Paradise

But turned back
Since I left
My sunscreen

And sunburns
Hurt worse when
You're alone.

Carol L. Gloor – *2nd Place, Adult Non-Resident*

Apple River Canyon

We bring our
bones to this
golden stream,

shed shoes that
smell Winter,
navigate

together,
hold old hands,
cross to Spring.

Max Pass - *2nd Place, 4th Grade Student*

Snowman

My snowman
Someone nice
Cold as ice

While he stood
I observe
Him standing

Dawn to dusk
Standing tall
Watching all

Sammi Hoffberg – *2nd Place, 5th Grade Student*

YouTube

Ads are dumb
Copyright
Clickbaits trash

Gamers game
Vloggers vlog
Pranksters prank

Don't forget
Two thumbs up
And subscribe!

Drake Elman - *3rd Place, 4th Grade Student*

I See the Woods

I see a
Waterfall
In the woods

I see trees
By the rock
Listening

To the calm
Waterfall
Peace at last

Noah Carson – *3rd Place, 5th Grade Student*

Earth

Earth will die
I won't lie
Please help it

Or I'll cry
Don't spread hate
Earth is great

Don't throw trash,
Or you'll turn
Into ash

Marjorie Rissman – *3rd Place, Highland Park Resident*

New Year Dream

Christmas tree
bright with lights
warms the night.

Too soon gone
to curbside
pick up truck.

Chopped to chips
ground to mulch
waits for spring.

Wilda Morris – *3rd Place, Adult Non-Resident*

In San Miguel de Allende, 2007

In an old
Mexican
bar I gape

at bull heads
and branding
irons and

sympathize
with Francis,
statued saint

Merle Tovian – *Honorable Mention, Highland Park Resident*

Sheltering

Sky-blue hut
pine smelling
stalks rustling

Leaves of oak,
red maple,
green cedar

Harvesting
the year and
my prayers.

Emma Alexandra – *Honorable Mention, Highland Park Resident*

Nature's Dance

Chickadee's
sixteen calls
repertoire

signals love,
bird feeders filled,
hawk sightings,

quick flights
nature's dance,
its wisdom.

Kathleen A. Lawrence – *Honorable Mention, Adult Non-Resident*

What to Do?

Three minutes
isn't long
to express

my cold fears
and boiling
hot desires.

Just enough
time for my
to do list.

Jan Chronister – *Honorable Mention, Adult Non-Resident*

All That Remains

abandoned
stalks of corn
forgotten

ragged men
with their backs
to the wind

burnished oaks
drained of wine
wait for spring

Addison Dickman – *Honorable Mention, 5th Grade Student*

Hoover

He is soft.
And playful.
Woof! Woof! Woof!

I love him.
He cuddles.
Woof! Woof! Woof!

Little dog.
Big people.
Woof! Woof! Woof!

Shayna Itkin – *Honorable Mention, 5th Grade Student*

Cake is Great

I like cake
Cake is great
But it gives

Stomachaches
I like cake
It is sweet

It is like
A cakey
Candy treat

Eden Bernardi – *Honorable Mention, 4th Grade Student*

A Girl's Game

Basketball
A girl's game
Bringing change

Feel the sweat
Beat the rest
Be the best

Three point shots
When your hot
Swish, jumpshot!

Valentina Di Martino – *Honorable Mention, 4th Grade Student*

Strange Animals

Pandas that
Eat pizza
Are awesome

Tigers that
Ride surfboards
Are so cool

Penguins that
Run real weird
Are crazy

Sadie Weissman - *Honorable Mention, 4th Grade Student*

Animals

Chimpanzees
Are very
Curious

Tigers are
Very brave
And so fast

But humans
Are the best
Don't ya think?

ABOUT THE JUDGES

Chemistry
Laura Potts is twenty-two years old and lives in West Yorkshire, England. Twice-recipient of the Foyle Young Poets Award, her work has been published by *Aesthetica, The Moth* and *The Poetry Business*. Having worked at The Dylan Thomas Birthplace in Swansea, Laura was nominated for The Pushcart Prize and became one of the BBC's New Voices last year. Her first BBC radio drama aired at Christmas. She received a commendation from The Poetry Society in 2018.

L. Frank Baum's Land of Oz
Sylvia Riojas Vaughn of Plano, Texas, worked as a journalist and a certified ESL teacher after graduating from Southern Methodist University. A Pushcart Prize and Best of the Net Nominee, she has been selected three times as a Houston Poetry Fest Juried Poet, and was named a Waco Wordfest Distinguished Writer in 2017. She learned poetic craftsmanship with the Dallas Poets Community.

Tricube Poems
Sofia M. Starnes, Virginia Poet Laureate from 2012 to 2014, is the author of six poetry collections, most recently *The Consequence of Moonlight* (Paraclete Press, 2018). She is also the recipient of a Poetry Fellowship from the Virginia Commission for the Arts, among other commendations, including five Pushcart Prize nominations and a D. of Letters degree (*honoris causa*) from Union College, Kentucky. Sofia serves as Poetry Editor and Poetry Book Review Editor of *The Anglican Theological Review*. For more information, please visit www.sofiamstarnes.com.

38851756R00044

Made in the USA
Middletown, DE
16 March 2019